Pebble™ Plus

A Visit to

The Doctor's Office

by B. A. Hoena

Consulting Editor: Gail Saunders-Smith, Ph.D.

Reading Consultant: Jennifer Norford, Senior Consultant
Mid-continent Research for Education and Learning
Aurora, Colorado

Capstone press

Mankato, Minnesota

Pebble Plus is published by Capstone Press
151 Good Counsel Drive, P.O. Box 669, Mankato, Minnesota 56002
www.capstonepress.com

1 2 3 4 5 6 09 08 07 06 05 04

Library of Congress Cataloging-in-Publication Data
Hoena, B. A.
The doctor's office/by B. A. Hoena.
p. cm.—(Pebble plus, A visit to)
Includes bibliographical references and index.
Contents: The doctor's office—Around the office—The exam room—The lab—Staying healthy.
ISBN 0-7368-2391-3 (hardcover)
1. Physicians—Juvenile literature. 2. Medicine—Juvenile literature. 3. Children—Preparation for medical
care—Juvenile literature. [1. Physicians. 2. Medicine. 3. Medical care.] I. Title. II. Series.
R690.H577
610—dc22   2003011897

Editorial Credits
Sarah L. Schuette, editor; Jennifer Bergstrom, series designer; Karen Risch, product planning editor

Photo Credits
Capstone Press/Gary Sundermeyer, front cover (doctor, exam table), back cover, 1, 4–5, 6–7, 9, 11, 13, 14–15,
    17, 19, 20–21
PhotoDisc Inc., front cover (scale)

Pebble Plus thanks the Health Services Department at Minnesota State University, Mankato, for allowing us to
use their facility for photo shoots.

Note to Parents and Teachers

The series A Visit to supports national social studies standards related to the production, distribution, and consumption of goods and services. This book describes and illustrates a visit to a doctor's office. The images support early readers in understanding the text. The repetition of words and phrases helps early readers learn new words. This book also introduces early readers to subject-specific vocabulary words, which are defined in the Glossary section. Early readers may need assistance to read some words and to use the Table of Contents, Glossary, Read More, Internet Sites, and Index/Word List sections of the book.

Word Count: 127
Early-Intervention Level: 16

Table of Contents

The Doctor's Office

A doctor's office is a busy place to visit. People go to the doctor's office when they are sick or need a checkup.

People sit in the waiting
room. They wait to see
a doctor or a nurse.

Around the Office

Office workers keep records
and make appointments.
They file charts and answer
the phones.

Nurses help patients get
ready to see a doctor.
Nurses write down how
much each patient weighs.

Doctors write prescriptions
and read charts.

The Exam Room

Patients see their doctor
in the exam room.
The patient sits on a table
during an exam.

15

Instruments help doctors and

nurses check their patients.

The Lab

Lab workers do tests
in the lab. Gloves keep
their hands clean and safe.

Staying Healthy

People visit the doctor's office to help them feel better and stay healthy.

Glossary

appointment—an arrangement to meet someone at a certain time

chart—the place where information about a patient is kept; information is added to a chart each time a patient visits the doctor's office.

exam room—a room where doctors and nurses check the health of a patient; another word for exam is examination.

instrument—a medical tool used to examine or treat patients

lab—a room with equipment that is used to do scientific tests; another word for lab is laboratory.

patient—a person who is cared for by a doctor or a nurse

prescription—a written order for medicine

Read More

Gorman, Jacqueline Laks. *Doctor.* People in My Community. Milwaukee: Weekly Reader Early Learning Library, 2002.

Schaefer, Lola M. *We Need Doctors.* Helpers in Our Community. Mankato, Minn.: Pebble Books, 2000.

Snyder, Inez. *Doctor Tools.* Tools. New York: Children's Press, 2002.

Internet Sites

FactHound offers a safe, fun way to find Internet sites related to this book. All of the sites on FactHound have been researched by our staff.

Here's how:

1. Visit *www.facthound.com*

2. Type in this special code **0736823913** for age-appropriate sites. Or enter a search word related to this book for a more general search.

3. Click on the Fetch It button.

FactHound will fetch the best sites for you!

Index/Word List